The
Quotable
Stoic

~:~

The Quotable Stoic

A Book of Original Aphorisms

Michael Lipsey

LOST
COAST
PRESS

The Quotable Stoic
A Book of Original Aphorisms
Copyright ©2014 by Michael Lipsey

Lost Coast Press
155 Cypress Street
Fort Bragg, CA 95437
(800) 773-7782
www.cypresshouse.com

Cover and book design: M.L. Brechner / Cypress House

Library of Congress Control Number: 2012950517

ISBN 978-1-935448-23-5

Printed in the USA
2 4 6 8 9 7 5 3 1

To my wife Louise Kanter Lipsey
who proudly insists that I'm a philosopher —
well, I'll give that some thought.

～:～

Do not let yourself
be deluded by anyone;
this is all I teach.
— Rinzai

～:～

Mind, like parachute,
only function when open.
— Charlie Chan

～:～

When people talk, listen completely.
Most people never listen.
— Ernest Hemingway

～:～

My day passes between logic,
whistling, going for walks, and being
depressed.
— Ludwig Wittgenstein

～:～

Table of Contents

Introduction

The hardest part of a career writing epigrams has been learning to introduce myself as an epigrammatist without stumbling over the word. At a party someone asks, "So, what do you do?" Pause. Deep breath. "I'm an epigrammatist."

"So what is a … did you say enigmatatist?"

~:~

A man's character is his fate.
— Heraclitus

~:~

A very large thought condensed into a mere six words, but perhaps the greatest of all epigrams. Taking a larger view you might say that karma is the same concept. The task of an epigrammatist is finding the exact, perfect word that completes the thought. I've written 1,500 epigrams, but I doubt I will hatch anything approaching these words of Heraclitus.

In college I discovered philosophy, and most especially, Stoicism. I've found Epictetus, Zeno of Citium, Seneca, Wittgenstein, Rousseau, Schopenhauer, and the rest of the questioning herd useful guides as I made my way through the ups and downs of the following decades of my life.

Philosophy has been described as an attempt to discover how to live. On the other hand, Ludwig Wittgenstein thought it more a kind of therapy.

࿓

*What can be said at all can be said clearly, and what
we cannot talk about we must pass over in silence.*
— Wittgenstein

࿓

It takes myriad forms, from folk proverbs to impenetrable sym-
bol-laden academic jargon. It can be easy to read and impossible
to read, and the ideas and schools of philosophy are maddeningly
difficult to remember. Still, I've found good reasons to drink from
these wells again and again. My epigrams are attempts to distill
the larger problems of life into as few words as possible. In finding the keys to living a decent life it is often enough to simply ask
the questions.

࿓

*I hate and renounce as a coward every being who cannot think that
the search for his life as a being is a study superior to that of giving
himself over to sensations or to notions lent by other personalities.*
— Antonin Artaud

࿓

What are the things we wonder about? Am I programmed to
behave in certain ways? Will something of me still exist when I
die? Do I really have choices? Why are some people always happy
and others unhappy? Are criminals truly evil? Is there a purpose
to my life? Are people everywhere fundamentally the same? Does
everyone feel like a failure? Who are my true friends? What is
true friendship? Is my religion truer than some others? Is there
any truth to religion?

Do animals have rights? Should suicide be permitted? Should psychopaths be executed? Is the news just propaganda? Should I give till it hurts? At what point do I go from being responsible for my children to expecting my children to be responsible for me? Would I actually be happier if I had more money? How well do I really know my friends?

꞊ː꞉

Wicked men have only accomplices, revelers have only partners, businessmen have only associates, politicians assemble only factions, ordinary loafers have only companions, and princes have only courtesans; virtuous men alone have friends.
— Voltaire

꞊ː꞉

Why do I feel as if no one is really hearing me? Is there progress or are we going backward? What were my ancestors really like? How do other people see me? What is love, and why does it last or not? Was there ever a good government? Am I unique? Do physicists really know anything about the material world?

꞊ː꞉

I think the universe is all spots and jumps, without unity, without continuity, without coherence or orderliness or any of the other properties that governesses love.
— Bertrand Russell

꞊ː꞉

Philosophy endlessly asks the most fundamental questions. You could say that it is the only discipline that does not progress, because the problems of life are always the same, once our basic material needs have been met. There may not be definitive

answers to these questions, but by asking them we may find ways
to find our way.

⁓:⁓

If, as they say, I am only an ignorant man trying to be a
philosopher, then that may be what a philosopher is.
— Diogenes

⁓:⁓

I'm not so arrogant as to call myself a philosopher — only a
seeker and a questioner. I question authority and why the streets
of my suburb are laid out as they are. I question my patriotism,
my faith, and whether I am a decent human being. I'm interested in everything, because there are patterns and meanings in
everything around us. As I write there's a frog croaking behind
a bookcase in my office. Why did he go to the bother of finding
a way into my house? Is he croaking for me to find him and put
him back outside, or croaking to attract a mate, or to warn other
males that this is his territory? And is this introduction just more
of my croaking? What can I expect to gain from this croaking?

⁓:⁓

I have seen born, pass and die many schools and promoters of
ephemera — Pointillists, Impressionists, Cubists, Futurists, etc.,
etc.... And so, I have cried with all my lungs: The louder these
bullfrogs croak the closer they are to bursting. My friends,
works of a personal vision alone will live.
— James Ensor, 1923

⁓:⁓

I see reality as more like a kaleidoscope than a telescope or micro-
scope, because whatever this thing we call reality is, we view it
only through a lens of our prejudices and preconceptions. The

hardest thing in the world is to simply see what you are looking at and to hear what you are hearing. And to just feel what you are feeling. If we are seekers, we can spend a lifetime trying to understand our own natures.

⌒⋮⌏

I have nothing but myself to write about, and this self that I have,
I hardly know of what it consists.
— Rousseau

⌒⋮⌏

Our societies are prolific machines that hum along, turning out saints, sinners and psychopaths, lovers and haters, happy and miserable families, enterprise and failure, kindness and cruelty, workaholics and slackers, schemers and dreamers, cults and crazes, despots and democrats, idiots and geniuses, gourmets and gluttons, believers and atheists, the pure of heart and the depraved, ascetics and addicts, bible study groups, bridge clubs, and genocides. We have more individuation than other species.

Nature we both understand and do not understand at all. We dissect a frog in high school, or send a telescope into space to search for the origin and limits of the universe, classify hundreds of thousands of species of beetles. On the other hand, we know nothing of what, why, or how it all came about. We have science, and we also have a great mystery that will always be beyond human understanding.

⌒⋮⌏

Man is forever talking about life, man and art. But he knows no
more than the mushroom what life, man and art actually are.
— Hans Arp

⌒⋮⌏

I consider myself both an artist and a writer, putting as much effort into creating collages using my epigrams as I do arranging them for books. I would rather have been William Blake than Socrates. Regarding originality, I doubt that I am the first to say anything. My epigrams are original to the best of my ability, but I'm not so arrogant as to imagine that I've thought of something that hasn't already been said, in someone else's words, last year or on a porch in Athens, 450 BC.

All my best thoughts were stolen by the ancients.
— Ralph Waldo Emerson

You might be surprised to learn that I have a system for composing epigrams. The Waste Book method of writing was invented by Georg Christoph Lichtenberg in the 18th century. I am also grateful for Carolyn See's *Making a Literary Life* and her thousand-word-a-day program. Writing is a muscle, and it gets stronger with use and weaker with disuse. I promise you, aspiring writer — whether of mysteries, histories, erotica, neurotica, elegies or rap — that if you write a thousand words a day, seven days a week, for the rest of your life, you will at least get very good at the writing part of writing. But as for the reason you are a writer, the stories, novels, history, poems, essays, your unique message for humanity, only the gods can help you.

Am I a serious artist, single-mindedly devoted to a search for truth? Let's just say that if you aren't laughing at the absurdity of it all, you've already got one foot in the grave. Life is about having fun, and I write and paint because creative work gives me pleasure. I get the same pleasure from my gardening, though it requires contending with all of nature's dirty tricks. I spare myself the illusion that by my writing I am imparting wisdom, improving humanity, or leaving some kind of legacy. We are what we are, and the thing is to make the most of ourselves, given whatever gifts we may possess.

꧁꧂

A very important thing is not to make up
your mind that you are any one thing.
— Gertrude Stein

꧁꧂

Epigrams are useful, hardworking prose. They can convey wisdom and quick moral lessons. They add polish to a speech, make points in a debate, and add sizzle to a business presentation. You can build a toast around one at a wedding or anniversary party. They teach philosophy. They say something we can't quite put into words ourselves. They save time and explanations. Literally millions of blogs are quoting epigrams every day as text or text over photos or illustrations. You probably use one in conversation almost every day, and have another appear in your mind as often. I wish you as much pleasure in reading my epigrams as I had in writing them.

꧁꧂

The world we live in is the words we use.
— Wittgenstein

꧁꧂

❦

Just because your closest friends
are those to whom you can tell
everything doesn't mean
that you should.

❦

Let the other person
complete the thought
before you open your yap.

❦

When half the guests
have gone home,
be among them.

❦

~:~

A gourmet is always at war
with his inner glutton.

~:~

No one duller than someone who makes
a pun or a joke out of everything.

~:~

We can easily improve our
appearance, manners, and behavior —
the personality is a little tougher.

~:~

There is an imaginary person
we speak of named "one" who is
usually a very good or very bad
example of something.

~:~

To rise in society, the first thing
you need to work on
is your laugh.

~:~

~:~

The most unpleasant people
seem to have a knack for saying
unpleasant things pleasantly.

~:~

When offended, think a long moment
before responding, to be sure you
haven't misunderstood something.

~:~

If you are a decent person, you suffer
when you realize that you've been unkind.

~:~

It isn't offensive to be politically
incorrect, unless you take
pride in being so.

~:~

There is an art to listening
intently without disconcerting the
speaker with an unblinking stare.

~:~

~:~

Why no disability rights
for the socially challenged?

~:~

Being a very poor listener is
nearly as serious a handicap as
being profoundly deaf.

~:~

Don't assume that your friends
are rude for not introducing
you — assume that they can't
remember your name.

~:~

Punning is sometimes a form of
hostility, reducing the words of
others to nonsense and making
serious conversation impossible.

~:~

⁓:⁓

Conversationalists can be
divided into generalists and
specialists — the former find the
latter boring, and the latter find
the former shallow.

⁓:⁓

Social ineptitude is often a
matter of not being able
to take a hint.

⁓:⁓

There was a time when shameless
self-promotion was bad form.

⁓:⁓

I can't say that having made the
effort to get to know an unfriendly
person was ever worth the effort.

⁓:⁓

∼:∼

Don't say, "You must" when
giving advice — because that
turns the advice into an order.

∼:∼

We all want to be heard,
but few want to listen.

∼:∼

Charismatic people have
something that is more animal
than human — like the beauty of
a horse, the poise of a cat, or the
deadly fascination of a snake.

∼:∼

Are you aware that you can
accumulate Courtesy Karma?

∼:∼

∾:∾

Life in Cell Phone Liar Nation:
"Sorry, I have to take this call."
Liar.

∾:∾

We Americans believe that
people should mind their own
business, even though most of
us have very little of it.

∾:∾

Extreme personalities really don't
mind making fools of themselves.

∾:∾

Making an impression is always
easy — making a good one is
somewhat harder.

∾:∾

∽:∾

Lying is always bad, but there's nothing
wrong with changing the subject.

∽:∾

At the lower levels of society, having a
big mouth is often a fatal condition.

∽:∾

A poor listener passes through life
without ever experiencing
a real conversation.

∽:∾

The less personality someone has, the
harder it is to remember his name or
his face, or her name *and* her face —
so with such persons one must make a
greater effort to latch onto something
memorable about them, even if it is
only a shy smile or retro eyeglasses.

∽:∾

~:~

Happiness is that cheap drug
that can be plucked from the air.

~:~

I don't care to know my place.

~:~

Go to successful people for
advice, because they don't think
in terms of failure.

~:~

You really only need to keep one
mood on hand, a good one — you
can get rid of all the rest.

~:~

∾⦂∿

A good disposition sails
merrily through a sea of bad
dispositions.

∾⦂∿

Stop apologizing for things that
aren't your fault.

∾⦂∿

I've never invented anything,
except myself.

∾⦂∿

Self-pity won't even get you out
of the starting gate.

∾⦂∿

By all honorable means, rise far
above your circumstances.

∾⦂∿

~:~

How do you know it's "no" if
you haven't even asked?

~:~

Good things happening in your
life aren't worth much if you
don't feel worthy of them.

~:~

You are a victim of everything
you believe you're a victim
of — whether it is true or not.

~:~

Sometimes when I'm pissed off about
something I look out the window and
see that the world is smiling at me.

~:~

~:~

The things that bother us the
most are usually the things that
matter the least.

~:~

Maintaining a good attitude requires
a lot of maintenance — but a bad
attitude is maintenance free.

~:~

I've been blessed with an
abundance of sheer amazement.

~:~

The true complainer is capable
of complaining even while
having a good time.

~:~

You can't be disillusioned if you've
never had any illusions — but that
wouldn't be good either.

~:~

∾:∾

A sweet personality on a homely
face is still more attractive than
a surly one on a pretty face.

∾:∾

Boredom is an inability to
appreciate what is happening at the
moment — and something always is.

∾:∾

There's nothing wrong with
resenting ingratitude.

∾:∾

Seeing a celebrity is a big deal if you think
of yourself as a person of no consequence.

∾:∾

Life is full of insignificant
disappointments.

∾:∾

~:~

When your mind is going at a
million miles an hour
it's going nowhere.

~:~

It is nearly impossible to think
and be angry at the same time.

~:~

Low expectations are seldom
disappointed, but high
expectations are often fulfilled.

~:~

They say, "You never learn, do you?"
I say, "My rules or theirs?"

~:~

~:~

If I hit the ground running
will you help me up?

~:~

Most of us feel like misfits as
teenagers, but then there are
those few who are convinced
that the world is the misfit.

~:~

Pessimism comes from thinking too
much, optimism from too little.

~:~

Don't accept blame for the things
that aren't your fault — and don't
make excuses for the things that are.

~:~

~:~

Attitude is 50 percent of your
reality — unfortunately, reality
is the other 50 percent

~:~

Bragging serves mainly to
reveal your low self-esteem.

~:~

There are some awful things about
human nature. Just to give one
example, it is ten times easier for us
to be critical than to be supportive.

~:~

⁓:⁓

At a low point in your life you decide
to make some serious changes —
and that moment turns out to
be a high point in your life.

⁓:⁓

I'm amazed by a lot of
things — but there's very little
that surprises me.

⁓:⁓

There were so many things on
my mind that my brain had to
start taking numbers.

⁓:⁓

~:~

Have you ever wondered what
life was like... yesterday?

~:~

Of those who hit bottom, some
have fallen a lot farther than
others, but it's the same bottom.

~:~

You can find a way through many
difficult situations in life if you can
just remember to breathe.

~:~

We can have well-organized
offices and well-organized
homes, but we can't have well-
organized minds.

~:~

~:~

The tragedy of contemporary
life is the loss of attention span.

~:~

You don't follow a serious
interest — it drives you.

~:~

A foolish person goes through
life at the mercy of events and
the luck of the draw.

~:~

You have to ignore a lot of
crossing signals on your way to a
personal train wreck.

~:~

∾:∾

Each day is an intricate
web of things done and left
undone — woven together by our
attention and our inattention.

∾:∾

One day I will get everything
done I planned to do — also on
that day the Messiah will come.

∾:∾

You are molded by your
formative experiences — but you
shouldn't be cast in stone.

∾:∾

Quiet minutes make quiet hours,
quiet hours make quiet days,
quiet days make a quiet life.

∾:∾

~:~

The passing traffic is passing
minds, full of thoughts.

~:~

Get advice from people who are
smarter than you, and never assume
that you're smarter than others.

~:~

One of the bigger mistakes you
can make in life is assuming that
everyone has a sense of humor.

~:~

People brag about being extremely
busy — as if it were more an
accomplishment than a waste of life.

~:~

~:~

We all procrastinate, but a truly
great procrastinator spends his
entire life getting ready.

~:~

You accomplish very little of
what you intended to accomplish
in life — but if you manage to
accomplish even that little,
you are regarded as a person
of accomplishments.

~:~

You might not be able to
improve your personality, but
you can certainly improve your
behavior, and that will work
almost as well.

~:~

∼:∼

Few lack a talent for the
art of procrastination.

∼:∼

Everything is random, but some
days feel more random.

∼:∼

Sports metaphors are seldom
apt, because life is not a game.

∼:∼

After false starts, blind alleys, dead
ends, and wrong turns, somehow
I managed to become the person I
wanted to be — no thanks to the map.

∼:∼

~:~

You have to come to terms with
the terms of your contract
with the universe.

~:~

No need to worry —
life is a temporary condition
that soon passes.

~:~

Ask yourself what you are truly
interested in, and let the rest fall away.

~:~

Nothing unexpected that
happens in your life compares to
the shock of being born.

~:~

∼:∼

I counted my blessings,
deducted my curses, and was
glad to see a positive balance.

∼:∼

The more highly scheduled your
life — the less it is a life.

∼:∼

We should hope that life is
kinder to kind people.

∼:∼

Your excuses for what has not gone
well in your life are like rubber
crutches: you can't stand on them.

∼:∼

∼:∼

Those who feel they've made a
great success of their lives were
generally not so ambitious.

∼:∼

You get to spend your entire life,
but at least you don't have to pay
it back.

∼:∼

Deal with what you are capable
of dealing with, and let others
deal with the rest.

∼:∼

If you have poor judgment,
there's nothing worse than being
decisive.

∼:∼

∼:∼

Father Death is not my friend
yet, but I hope to live long
enough that a time will come
when he will be.

∼:∼

Old bones feel older in winter.

∼:∼

A good doctor never forgets that
the patient is a person.

∼:∼

Choose your last words
carefully — you won't be able to
take them back.

∼:∼

~:~

An emergency room sees the
results of many varieties
of poor judgment.

~:~

You aren't really, truly an adult
until you have written a will.

~:~

I would imagine that surgeons fear
having surgery the most, knowing
the consequences of a moment of
inattention or a slip of the knife.

~:~

Emergencies never seem real.

~:~

～:～

Our most insincere moments
are the forced cheerfulness we
produce in the face of bad news.

～:～

A nice big compost bin with
plenty of worms would make a
fine grave.

～:～

The expectation of bad news
causes a general paralysis of the
mind.

～:～

Obsessive thinking will eventually
wear a hole in your mind.

～:～

~:~

When recklessness puts you in
the ditch, don't call it an accident.

~:~

There's no harm in allowing a
modest amount of melancholy
into your life.

~:~

We feel uncomfortable in the
presence of the insane because
of a not entirely irrational fear of
contagion.

~:~

I'm finally getting comfortable
with the idea of being old — the
next hurdle will be getting used
to the idea of being really old.

~:~

~:~

My stomach doesn't seem to give
a damn about the welfare of the
rest of my body.

~:~

I have many cruel
masters — coffee, for example.

~:~

When you're too tired to think,
you realize that your brain is
just another part of your body.

~:~

While having the second piece
of cake we think that we really
shouldn't — but the thought does
not encompass an early death from
heart disease or diabetes.

~:~

～:～

Major purchase anxiety —
a personality disorder that
eventually passes without need
of treatment.

～:～

Honestly, what is the ratio of
the fruit that you buy to the
fruit that you actually eat?

～:～

I will be done before
my work will.

～:～

The problem of obesity could be solved
if a drug was developed that made
being a little hungry sexually arousing.

～:～

⌁⦂⦉

Lizzie Borden, patron saint of
those who care for elderly parents.

⌁⦂⦉

My funeral instruction: scatter
ashes downwind.

⌁⦂⦉

If you don't want to injure
yourself, don't reach for
anything that isn't within reach.

⌁⦂⦉

I'm convinced that I've got some
rare disease only about once a
month — but dementia, daily!

⌁⦂⦉

∽:∽

The word "burn" should be
substituted for the word "tan." As in
"Burning Salon," or "I think a nice
burn looks good in winter."

∽:∽

Every religion tries
to sugarcoat death.

∽:∽

An older person with very
elderly parents can go from
being a caretaker to needing a
caretaker in just a few years.

∽:∽

As you get older, an age-appropriate
diet will save you a lot of grief.
That is the extent of my advice.

∽:∽

～:～

A sensible old age is a maximum
of fun within the limits of what
is possible, with no regrets
regarding what isn't.

～:～

We spend the rest of the new year
dealing with the consequences of
the permissions we gave ourselves
over the holidays.

～:～

We take secrets to our graves
that are no big deal to anyone
but ourselves.

～:～

I'd like the last chapter of my life to
be like a good read that you enjoyed
to the end and were sorry to finish.

～:～

∾∶∽

I truly believe that exercise is making
me healthier — but knowing it is
partly due to the exercise and
partly due to the believing.

∾∶∽

Many accidents could more
properly be called "inattentions."

∾∶∽

If your personality doesn't
improve when you drink,
you are probably a drunk.

∾∶∽

A healthy-minded person
doesn't think about death more
times a day than their age.

∾∶∽

~:~

Hypochondria is unique among
mental disorders in that it is based
on an underlying reality —
that we all sicken and die.

~:~

We Americans are such a health-
obsessed, unhealthy nation.

~:~

We can joke about someone
being high maintenance, but we
all become high maintenance
when we get old.

~:~

Not content with merely
trying to kill you, the illness may
attempt to become your identity.

~:~

~:~

Routine is good, but if you want to stay
young, try something new every day.

~:~

Luxury travel
broadens our behinds.

~:~

You begin to view your life with
a bit of distance as you get older,
and with a lot more distance
when you get really old.

~:~

༄:༅

When I am ninety, if the
memory of twenty is more vivid
than that of eighty-nine, you
won't hear me complaining.

༄:༅

At a class reunion we ransack our
memories for something, anything,
about this person who is talking to us.

༄:༅

Like a tree growing rings, every year
brings another dimension to our lives.

༄:༅

⌒:⁓

Accepting your age doesn't
mean you must act like it.

⌒:⁓

In the dream world everything
is at the same time, and
everywhere is right next to
everywhere else.

⌒:⁓

We do not fully appreciate the
comforts of our daily routine
until something disrupts it.

⌒:⁓

At what age does one stop looking
forward to one's birthday?

⌒:⁓

᙭

Nostalgia is remembering
only the good parts.

᙭

We must rely on our memory,
even though we know it is not
to be trusted.

᙭

There are entire years of my life I
can't account for — but that doesn't
mean they weren't eventful.

᙭

Sometimes you remember the
expression before you recognize
the face it is on.

᙭

～:～

There might be the same
amount of time in each hour,
day and year — but it sure
doesn't feel like it.

～:～

Best to peak late in life — and
worst to peak in high school.

～:～

Having a great idea and then not
being able to remember what it
was — absolutely maddening!

～:～

You have to become old, but you
don't have to become stubborn,
grouchy, and difficult.

～:～

∽:∽

After a certain age, *anything* you
can't remember is grounds
for a panic attack.

∽:∽

You can measure your life
in hours, days, and years —
or you can measure it
in accomplishments.

∽:∽

What we call an eternity is usually
just a few impatient minutes.

∽:∽

We exchange our time for money, and
our money for goods — too bad that
we can't exchange the goods for time.

∽:∽

~:~

My mind cannot begin to
encompass everything that
happens in even a typical day.

~:~

After a certain age, it takes a
considerable effort of will to not
turn into a curmudgeon.

~:~

There comes a time when you can
either be old, or be ridiculous.

~:~

Never go to the grocery store
without a list, even for only
three items. Two. One.

~:~

～:～

One of the few benefits of getting
older is that your excuses for getting
out of stuff become more plausible.

～:～

On the plus side, a poor memory
does free brain capacity for thinking
new and interesting thoughts.

～:～

Our travels occur in one world, and
the memories of them in another.

～:～

At sixteen nothing seems more
wonderful than being popular; at
sixty nothing seems more annoying.

～:～

~:~

When maturity is a very long time
coming, senility may not be far behind.

~:~

When implanted human memory
becomes a commodity like computer
memory, how much memory would
you want? Would you like to
remember every minute of your life?
NO!

~:~

There is a tipping point in midlife,
a day when you feel that middle-
ness of having equal parts past and
future, of the life that you've lived
and the life that you will live, of what
is finished and what is still possible.

~:~

༄༅

There's so much I'd like to
remember, that I've forgotten —
and there's so much I'd like to
forget that I keep remembering.

༄༅

The tattoos that adorn so many
young people are such sweet,
evocative symbols of future regrets.

༄༅

When you are the last person who
still remembers certain relatives,
your versions of family stories
become authoritative.

༄༅

~:~

Little thoughts crowd out the big ones.

~:~

Obsessive thinking is like
pedaling hard on a stationary
bicycle — it gets you nowhere.

~:~

In a difficult situation, a calm
voice is oil on troubled waters.

~:~

The test of time for wisdom is
measured in units of a thousand years.

~:~

❖

It was a genius idea —
until the next morning.

❖

Why does good judgment, the
thing that makes our lives go
well, come so easily to some
and never to others?

❖

Raw intelligence is like an
electrical socket: huge potential,
if only you have something
useful to plug into it.

❖

Phony wisdom —
it contaminates the mind.

❖

~:~

An exchange of opinion is always more
fruitful than a delivery of opinion.

~:~

Everything I was born knowing
was in my genes, except for a few
things I picked up in the womb.

~:~

You have to seek out good
advice, but bad advice is
freely available everywhere.

~:~

The real experts are very careful
with their opinions.

~:~

~:~

Phony wisdom is delivered with
a beautiful smile, as if to say,
look how simple it all is!

~:~

The problem with experience is
that each stage of your life offers
fresh possibilities for making
bad decisions.

~:~

Trying to teach students to
think brings the risk of merely
steeping them in the intellectual
fashions of the moment.

~:~

~:~

Being decisive does not
necessarily mean that you
are a good decision maker.

~:~

Brilliance needs direction —
or it scatters itself uselessly.

~:~

How much advice is wanted? Not
much. How much advice is taken?
Even less.

~:~

Profundity is that narrow
ridge between the chasms of
pomposity and idiocy.

~:~

∾∶∿

Act on the thoughts that crystallize,
not on the ones that congeal.

∾∶∿

I'll take an uneducated person of
common sense over any professor
whose head is filled with a thousand
subtleties and fine distinctions.

∾∶∿

The conventional wisdom is
safe, but there is very little
opportunity in it.

∾∶∿

When you've developed the
discipline to master one thing,
you have already acquired the
discipline to master others.

∾∶∿

~:~

Higher education generally
raises a person's intelligence,
but not by much.

~:~

The younger you get old enough
to know better, the better.

~:~

In real life, street smarts are often
worth more than intelligence.

~:~

Moments of complete concentration
are precious because the mind wants
to run off in all directions.

~:~

෴

Being a genius is hardly an
impediment to idiocy.

෴

When your only talent is
thinking you had better take
good care of your brain.

෴

Try not to have your greatest ideas in
the shower, because they'll be forgotten
before you can write them down.

෴

The human life span is much
too short to figure anything out.

෴

~:~

There are days when my mind is
a herd of cats trying to
herd a herd of cats.

~:~

Everyone thinks, but very few
think things through.

~:~

Random thoughts —
are there any other kind?

~:~

When my thoughts are like the
occasional car passing on a quiet street, I
have a certain clarity — but when they're
Los Angeles freeway rush hour, there's
nothing but the roar of traffic.

~:~

༆

A contrary contrarian believes
in the conventional wisdom.

༆

Don't worry — you can't think hard
enough to strain your brain.

༆

Our minds are a clutter of memories,
worries, desires, sensations, fantasies,
complaints, dreads, discomforts,
and annoyances — and even an
occasional thought.

༆

Friendship

~:~

It is often hard to tell whether a person is telling us something for a reason, or just babbling thoughtlessly.

~:~

There is crazy in a good way and there is crazy in a bad way — and they seldom intersect.

~:~

Some of the most useful people, the ones who challenge us the most, are also the most annoying.

~:~

∼:∼

The curmudgeon imagines that
people see through his gruff
facade to the goodhearted fellow
within — but they don't.

∼:∼

People who tell you about how
they have finally gotten over
something usually really haven't.

∼:∼

Your oldest friends may know
you the least because they
maintain a fixed image of the
person you once were.

∼:∼

Bars are good places to meet
people you later wish you hadn't.

∼:∼

~:~

We need a word for friends we
have no desire to see again, but
are always very interested in
hearing about.

~:~

Getting together with a friend
who has gone through life as a
time capsule of our college years
is a good way to revisit our youth.

~:~

It is possible to communicate certain
things just by means of eyebrows.

~:~

A nice part of hospitality is that
when it is over you don't have to
face the journey home.

~:~

∽:∼

The people at a community event that I like to meet aren't the ones who talked the most, but the ones who stayed after to put away the chairs and clean up.

∽:∼

Social life conducted by means of technology is lacking in nuance.

∽:∼

If you're into collecting, an inexpensive hobby is collecting nice people in your life.

∽:∼

In American culture, the word "friend" has so many meanings that it has almost no meaning.

∽:∼

~:~

We do best within a narrow
range of solitude, because too
much leaves us lonely, and too
little makes us crazy.

~:~

Think of how many people you
know, and then think of how
many people you *really* know.

~:~

Our crazier friends need to
offer a little more than our saner
friends to compensate us for the
bother of putting up with them.

~:~

Being warmly welcomed the first
time you go someplace makes
all the difference.

~:~

∽:∼

Very useful to be able to read
people — but unwise to
read them out loud.

∽:∼

Weigh advice from your
friends against how well they've
managed their own lives.

∽:∼

When meeting new people, ask
yourself, "Do I really need another
poor listener in my life?"

∽:∼

Just because your closest friends are
those to whom you can tell everything
doesn't mean that you should.

∽:∼

~:~

Is it possible that the people
who know me really well know
me better than I know myself?

~:~

You get to choose your friends, but
how wonderful it would be if you
could also choose your family!

~:~

Kill the urge to always say
something about yourself when
others say something personal.

~:~

The main difference between
interesting and dull people is
their degree of curiosity.

~:~

꘏ ꞉ ꘏

Scary being introduced, and
someone says, "Oh, I've heard *all*
about you!" It's never true, but just
the thought of it curdles the blood.

꘏ ꞉ ꘏

It's impossible to tease with a bit of
gossip — because your friends will
never let you go until they hear the rest.

꘏ ꞉ ꘏

I haven't noticed that my friends who
are constantly giving me health advice
are any healthier than the others.

꘏ ꞉ ꘏

When you realize that most of your
friends are strange, you need to come
to terms with the possibility —
no, make that the likelihood —
that you are strange.

꘏ ꞉ ꘏

Love

~:~

Our most complicated emotions are just combinations of simpler ones — like love and jealousy or gratitude and resentment.

~:~

If you think there is truth in proverbial wisdom, consider this old saw "No one ever died of love." Really? No suicides or crimes of passion?

~:~

If you really love someone, there isn't much that you aren't willing to put up with or work around — and if you really don't, there is much you won't put up with or try to work around.

~:~

~:~

Love has a lot of momentum; it
can feel like it's still going even
when it has already died.

~:~

Don't give relationship advice if
you aren't good at relationships.

~:~

There are times in life when a
brief relationship is not a failure,
but just what you needed to put
yourself back into circulation.

~:~

Doesn't matter if you are a
human, a sparrow, a whale, or a
cockroach — it's the sexy ones
who get the most affection.

~:~

∾:∽

There is no love where
there is no kindness.

∾:∽

There is a sweet spot between being
overly emotional and being unable to
access your emotions.

∾:∽

Saying bad things about the
person who dumped you just
makes you twice the loser.

∾:∽

There should be a word for the
feeling of regret that you missed
a chance mixed with relief that
you escaped the consequences
that might have followed.

∾:∽

~:~

You never get too old to flirt — just
too old for it to be taken seriously.

~:~

The commonest reason a woman
can't get a man to say much about
their relationship is that he simply
hasn't given it much thought.

~:~

Women find it hard to believe that
a man can go through life without
ever having a conversation with
another man analyzing his
relationship with a woman.

~:~

You're waiting to find
someone who is perfect for you?
So, are you perfect?

~:~

Some people fall asleep counting
sheep, others ex-lovers.

∾∶∾

When we talk about having a
full life we mean one that is full
of people you love, and people
who love you.

∾∶∾

Sometimes an impossible
relationship becomes possible, and
to everyone's amazement, endures
through the power of love.

∾∶∾

∽:∼

So much of popular culture is about
sex — and so little is about the erotic.

∽:∼

Guys hate relationship talk because
it invariably brings up questions for
which there are no right answers. To
put it in football terms, relationship
talk is a game in which the correct
play for every situation is punt.

∽:∼

Lingerie is about mysteries
being slightly revealed.

∽:∼

~:~

The good husband is willing to
be trained — the bad husband
wants to do the training.

~:~

Contrary to expert advice on
marital problems, it really is
possible to change the person
you married — you simply
divorce them and marry
someone else.

~:~

Many a shaky marriage is held
together by dogs and cats.

~:~

~:~

If you are having a hard time
choosing between advice from
your mother and advice from
your father, take your mother's.

~:~

Wouldn't it be nice if there were
a market in families, allowing
you to buy into another one or
sell your share in your own?

~:~

Every family produces a few
saints and scoundrels — and
the saints are usually more
unbearable than the scoundrels.

~:~

Divorce is that problem
that is also a solution.

~:~

~:~

With enough work, almost any
bad marriage can be saved —
the question is, why bother?

~:~

Each member of the family has
their very own dysfunctional
assigned role.

~:~

A man knows his life will
change when he gets married,
but he is not sure how.

~:~

Can it be that the impossible person
you married is also be married to
an impossible person?

~:~

❧

You own the universe until
you are judged capable of
understanding the word "No."

❧

The fundamental problem of
marriage is that although few
think of themselves in this way,
almost everyone is *really difficult.*

❧

Most of us are much crazier
with our family than we are
with our friends or at work.

❧

You have to have a family to truly
appreciate being home alone.

❧

꜌꞉ꜟ

One would imagine that a long-planned and ruinously expensive wedding would never end in an early divorce — but so often it does.

꜌꞉ꜟ

Why do we voluntarily accept all kinds of unnecessary obligations that consume so much of our hard-won free time?

꜌꞉ꜟ

When a hot person marries a cold person it is essential to have a comprehensive prenuptial thermostatic agreement.

꜌꞉ꜟ

Which wife was that who said I was incapable of change?

꜌꞉ꜟ

~:~

Speaking of polygamy, the idea
of coming home to two or three
wives who are all pissed off at
you is beyond imagining.

~:~

Imagine seeing yourself when
you're angry, and not liking what
you see.

~:~

You can't prevent family
craziness, but you can choose
not to participate in it.

~:~

When people gripe about their
spouses I often think, "and they
lived unhappily ever after."

~:~

∾:∾

In a large family gathering, you
can see what you once looked
like and you can see what you
are going to look like.

∾:∾

Why would I take marital advice
from someone who hasn't even been
married as many times as I have?

∾:∾

How many parents would make
sacrifices to send their children to college
simply from a love of knowledge?

∾:∾

The longer you've been divorced, the
stranger it seems that you could ever
have been married to that person.

∾:∾

∽:∼

All our lives we give our children
advice, without the least doubt
as to whether it is good advice.

∽:∼

The stupidest arguments
are usually the loudest.

∽:∼

A good marriage features
mutual management of
each other's craziness.

∽:∼

The teenager who doesn't feel
like a misfit is the misfit.

∽:∼

Contempt is the default state
of an abusive relationship.

∽:∼

∾:∾

The saddest divorce is one in
which neither partner ever finds
someone they like as much.

∾:∾

The main ingredient of keeping
passion alive is generosity, a desire
to give pleasure even stronger than
the desire to be pleasured.

∾:∾

Teenage pregnancy would fall
if teenagers could be convinced
that babies turn into teenagers.

∾:∾

One reason to have children is to learn
why you should forgive your parents, as
you inevitably discover how difficult, nearly
impossible, it is to be a really good one.

∾:∾

∼:∼

All things being equal, your
family is still more annoying
than your friends.

∼:∼

That a man is good at courtship
tells nothing about whether he
is good at relationships.

∼:∼

The child imagines that the adult has
all kinds of hidden powers — such as to
make pizza appear at the front door — so
the child is infuriated when the adult
refuses to use these unlimited hidden
powers to accommodate his wishes.

∼:∼

~:~

Traveling in a well-conducted tour
group is as close as an adult can
come to re-experiencing childhood.

~:~

A screaming grandchild
is much less disturbing than
your screaming child was.

~:~

A guy is more relaxed at his wedding
after he's had a few … weddings.

~:~

Ancient family grudges can
outlast any memory of the
original quarrel.

~:~

∽:∾

Take better care of your body than
of your house — the house will
outlive you without your help.

∽:∾

Never "try something" when you
have dinner guests — always
try it on yourself first.

∽:∾

After finally becoming a
suburbanite, I only regret having
spent so much of my life looking
for parking spaces.

∽:∾

❦

There are two kinds of pet owners:
those who own animals, and those
who have a furry family.

❦

We love to see wood in our homes
because it shows the infinitely varied
patterns of the natural thing that it is.

❦

That we Americans are
obsessed with home values is a sad
commentary on our lack of savings.

❦

I like to cook because I'm
incapable of cooking and
worrying at the same time.

❦

∾:∾

Channel surfing is a sport that has
always been dominated by men.

∾:∾

Gentrification is not something
that is done by the gentry.

∾:∾

When cabin fever strikes,
neither rain nor snow nor sleet
nor hail will keep us from
our un-appointed rounds of
unnecessary errands.

∾:∾

Consequences of very bad life
decisions sometimes manifest
themselves as smaller and
smaller living accommodations.

∾:∾

~:~

I must have put it somewhere —
well, everything is somewhere....

~:~

A scary neighborhood isn't
nearly as scary to the people
who actually live there.

~:~

They spent forty years fixing
up the place, and then a young
couple bought the house and
began the process all over again.

~:~

When you travel there is always
that moment in the night when
you are not sure where you are,
or why you're there.

~:~

∽:∽

Some very nice people sit on condo
boards only in self-defense.

∽:∽

To preserve sanity in a teeming
city one must learn to create
mental privacy.

∽:∽

You only need one room that
is your own, but it must
be totally your own.

∽:∽

You might not be very fond of
the locale you grew up in, but
it will always seem more real
to you than anyplace else.

∽:∽

❦

Every city has a ring, extending to
about a three-hour drive, in which rural
life is sustained by weekenders paying
for things the locals do themselves, do
without, or view as frivolities.

❦

A minimalist takes as much
pleasure in getting rid of stuff
as a clutter person does in
acquiring more of it.

❦

Cops now come with so much
stuff attached to their bodies it's
amazing they can even walk.

❦

Why is it there are always too
many, or too few, volunteers?

❦

~:~

Clumsy as we may be, we move gracefully
through the clutter of our homes.

~:~

At home you can be more
like yourself than you can be
anywhere else.

~:~

We are comfortable amidst our
own clutter, but uncomfortable
amidst anyone else's clutter.

~:~

If the organizational business often
takes up most of the meeting the
organization probably has
no good reason to exist.

~:~

~:~

You've made some very wise
investments — everything in your
house will be a valuable antique
in just a hundred years.

~:~

Urban renewal is simply about
removing a lot of people and
replacing them with a lot of other
people, but of a better class.

~:~

———————————

∾:∾

Try to persuade a trout
that fishing is a sport.

∾:∾

Spend a night alone in the woods
and you will see many things in the
periphery of your vision that aren't
there when you turn your head.

∾:∾

Think about cats, dogs, and ducks,
and then think about spiders, slugs,
and snakes — you weren't taught
the difference, it's in your DNA.

∾:∾

∽:∼

We are drawn to the shore, where
water and sky are joined at the eye.

∽:∼

From the viewpoint of the worm,
you are the one who ruins the apple.

∽:∼

We all want to save the planet,
but the planet could care less
about saving us.

∽:∼

What species will call us
endangered when we are on
the verge of extinction?

∽:∼

∾:∾

Your serious hiker is mainly
interested in covering as much
ground as possible.

∾:∾

It's bird watching or people
watching, depending on
which creature you are.

∾:∾

There is nothing the imagination
can produce that is as miraculous
as a hummingbird.

∾:∾

Very few people have a kinder
or more intelligent expression
than a golden retriever.

∾:∾

∾:∽

With so many improvements in
the ease and comfort of camping
it seems kind of pointless.

∾:∽

We are uncomfortable animals —
in the rare moments when we
get completely comfortable
we quickly fall asleep.

∾:∽

To raccoon society, the bungee
cords on our garbage cans are
like the velvet ropes in front of
an exclusive after-hours club.

∾:∽

I predict that when the final
chapter of evolution is written
we will be the house pets of
super-intelligent viruses.

∾:∽

~:~

One thing you can say about
humans: they build with as
much determination as ants.

~:~

I contemplate the universe
warmly — and the universe
contemplates me coldly.

~:~

Winter has more moods than the
other three seasons combined.

~:~

For every cell in my diminishing brain,
there is a galaxy in the universe —
about 100 billion in each case.

~:~

∽:∼

We would like to think that
our most intense pleasures are
intellectual, but in reality they are
those based on simple animal needs.

∽:∼

A dangerous warning behavior is a
tight little smile that may indicate
the human is about to attack.

∽:∼

I enjoy the melancholy of
a rainy dark wintry day in
spring — knowing it won't turn
into the depression of winter.

∽:∼

The good news is that we will
probably not be able to colonize
other planets, and so our destructive
nature will be confined to this one.

∽:∼

~:~

The landscape may be strange, but
the mind's landscape is even stranger.

~:~

A landscape exists only as a mental
construct — just as the mountains
we view as sublime were once seen
only as impediments to trade.

~:~

From the viewpoint of nature,
if nature had one, humans live
on uselessly, far longer than
their reproductive spans.

~:~

What do you call inviting a lot of
bugs to dinner? I call it a picnic.

~:~

~:~

The rider doesn't mind that the
horse doesn't know anything
better than being a horse.

~:~

A vampire is a kind of gigantic
mosquito that can fly though screens.

~:~

We thank God for having made
us intelligent animals — but not
that He made us animals.

~:~

We intellectuals are creatures that
dwell in forests that have been
harvested and turned into books.

~:~

∽:∼

In an organic garden
nature dines first.

∽:∼

People taking pictures at a
scenic overlook seldom take time
to just enjoy the view — nor are
they ever likely to find time to
look at the pictures.

∽:∼

There is always more to notice,
even if you live your entire life
in the same place.

∽:∼

As the mountain bluebirds are
winging their annual migration
from Mexico to Alaska, do they
ever ask each other, "Why don't we
just settle down in Santa Barbara?"

∽:∼

Science and Technology

⁓:⁓

That you are alive requires
thousands of miracles a minute.

⁓:⁓

I seem to have many good
evolutionary traits — not because I
am excellent, but because I am here.

⁓:⁓

Our experiments in the great laboratory
of human behavior are always
contaminated by our participation.

⁓:⁓

When I dive into the Internet I never
know when I'm going to come up for air.

⁓:⁓

∼:∼

The Theory of the *Schmutz* Universe:
It can be proven that the universe
is composed of schmutz, because
schmutz appears on your glasses in
the moment between cleaning them
and putting them back on your nose.

∼:∼

The Information Age will be followed
by the Enough Already! Age.

∼:∼

The number of neural connections in
your brain is roughly equivalent to the
entire Internet, and still you can't decide
which shirt to wear on your date?

∼:∼

Research has proven that most people
think they are smarter than they are and
better looking than they are — which
goes to prove that science is nasty.

∼:∼

⌒:∽

Cosmologically speaking, we need to
come up with something better than
science, religion and philosophy.

⌒:∽

When the genome is fully decoded, will
it contain genes for war and genocide?

⌒:∽

My great-great-great grandfather and
his brother walked from Moscow to
Budapest, and I'm trying to decide
whether to drive six blocks?

⌒:∽

Imagine a vast wind farm — powered
by American politicians and
French intellectuals.

⌒:∽

∾:∾

I'm developing an email program for
serious communicators. The letters will be
carved on stone tablets and delivered by
oxcart. It may be a bit slow, but a great deal
more thought will go into the messages.

∾:∾

Anyone considering a career in science
might note that few physicists will
discover a new particle, but most
entomologists will discover new species.

∾:∾

The controversy over stem cell
research will be nothing compared
to those regarding brain transplants,
cloned slaves, animal-human hybrids
and musicians with twenty fingers.

∾:∾

∾:∾

If the amount of information
were to be infinite, the ability to
make a decision would be zero.

∾:∾

The amount of information per exchange
is declining, as we communicate many
more times while not having more
information to communicate.

∾:∾

"In the Beginning there was…"
something that we will never
have a clue as to what it was.

∾:∾

Science is a search for
inescapable evidence.

∾:∾

~:~

The most reliable method of distinguishing
between a crank and a genius is to reevaluate
their work after a hundred years.

~:~

There are still more consequences
in real life, but virtual life is rapidly
gaining consequences.

~:~

We are becoming unequal to our own
inventions because we are incapable
of evolving quickly enough to keep
pace with science and technology.

~:~

The Internet is to librarians
as Gutenberg was to scribes.

~:~

❀

Weather made life possible, and weather will eventually make it impossible.

❀

A light bulb went off in Thomas Edison's head a thousand times before one appeared that worked outside of it.

❀

This end of privacy is going to take some getting used to.

❀

Life would be simpler to navigate if it came with drop-down menus.

❀

❦

On seeing a complete rainbow,
from horizon to horizon, for a few
minutes I become very religious.

❦

Einstein said that God
does not play dice with the
universe — could it be that
He is playing solitaire?

❦

Aspiring clergy are taught
to heighten meanings by
pronouncing certain words with
a peculiar emphasis never used
by ordinary worshippers.

❦

~:~

Suppose there really is an
intelligently designed God?

~:~

My religious views tend toward
the heretical, because that's
where the action is.

~:~

When the subject of religious
belief comes up we virtuously
recite our inoffensive, hedged,
vague and unexamined credos.

~:~

A nuclear war would be
a biblical event.

~:~

∾ःᵕ

We blame the gods for many things that
go wrong, but we only blame God when
the most terrible things happen to us.

∾ःᵕ

We believers always have the nagging
suspicion that the irreverent are
having more fun than the reverent.

∾ःᵕ

Ah, to be a supreme ayatollah or the
Dalai Lama or the pope, and know
what it feels like to be at the top of
the spiritual food chain!

∾ःᵕ

The real mystery is
everything, all of it.

∾ःᵕ

~:~

I worship God's better side.

~:~

If a celibate carried on a lively imaginary
sex life, would the celibacy be a fraud?

~:~

It would almost be worth going to
hell just to see what they do with the
souls of tobacco-industry lawyers.

~:~

Odd that the Christians have
proven themselves, of all major
world religions, the best at war.

~:~

A thinking believer ventures no
definitive statements about
the nature of God.

~:~

∼:∼

Saint Irony is the patron saint of
epigrammatists — he always answers
my prayers, but with a shrug.

∼:∼

One difference between
spirituality and religion is that
people are seldom tortured and
killed in the name of spirituality.

∼:∼

Our deep reverence for the martyrs
of our faith does not extend to the
martyrs of other faiths.

∼:∼

In matters of faith, the right
key might be small, but it can
unlock enormous doors.

∼:∼

~:~

We Jews were forbidden to make idols,
so we made an idol out of a book.

~:~

Clergy must pretend to greater
tolerance for other beliefs than
they have in their hearts.

~:~

In the contest between
religion and science, I wouldn't
necessarily recommend putting
your money on science.

~:~

The God that I worship is more
forgiving of sinners than of
hypocrites.

~:~

∾⦂∾

Aggravation is no friend
of contemplation.

∾⦂∾

Due to my heretical beliefs, I had no
choice but to excommunicate myself.

∾⦂∾

A split in a congregation is painful
for all, but a little less so for the side
that keeps the church.

∾⦂∾

Although America is a very religious
country, we avoid discussing social
problems in moral terms.

∾⦂∾

⌁∶⌁

Even a very supportive religious
community may from time to time
devour one of its own.

⌁∶⌁

I may not believe in the soul, but I do
believe there are things that offend my soul.

⌁∶⌁

Spirituality is heightened by ritual,
meditation, chanting, singing and
dancing — but diminished by
explanations and interpretations.

⌁∶⌁

A barbecue on any religious
holiday could also be considered
a biblical burnt offering.

⌁∶⌁

Never trust someone who says
you can trust them because of
their religious belief.

⌁∶⌁

∾:∾

The priestly caste always wants
to make the rules of society.

∾:∾

There's nothing wrong with making
a deal with the devil, unless of
course, it is actually true that you
have an immortal soul.

∾:∾

Religions are various combinations of
four cities: Jerusalem, Mecca, the Vatican
and Jonestown — the Imaginary City of
God, the place of pilgrimage, the dogmas
and hierarchy, and the Inquisition.

∾:∾

Fundamentalists resemble their counterparts
in other religions more than they resemble
their more liberal co-religionists.

∾:∾

~:~

I don't believe that I have a soul, but
it makes sense to behave as if I did.

~:~

There's no end to idolatry —
we make idols out of brands, athletes,
movie stars, billionaires, the flag, the
President and the Ten Commandments.

~:~

An example of God's sense of humor
is that He made the center of your
back the itchiest part of your body.

~:~

I pray: Dear Lord, let me be simple, but not
simpleminded. Complex but not complicated.
Self-confident but not overconfident. Thoughtful
but not obsessive. Courageous but not foolhardy.
Adventurous but not nuts. Loving but not
smothering. And humorous but not obnoxious.

~:~

⁓:⁓

Since it has taken me seventy years
just to begin to frame the questions,
I doubt if I will have time to get
to any of the answers.

⁓:⁓

If your father taught you what he learned
from his father, and so on — then you
come from a long line of Confucianists.

⁓:⁓

The logic of a lot of things is
inescapable, but that does not
prevent us from escaping it.

⁓:⁓

⌒:⌇

Philosophy, the poor
relation of common sense.

⌒:⌇

I have no idea, and then suddenly I
have an idea — what changed?

⌒:⌇

A philosopher is a question mark
dressed in human clothing.

⌒:⌇

Professors erect high walls around
small fields of knowledge.

⌒:⌇

Ancient historians believed that
nations decline because of a loss
of virtue — that holds up today.

⌒:⌇

~:~

If you can make your points by
asking questions you are
a modern Socrates.

~:~

When I was three I became
extremely curious, and that
stage of development has lasted
sixty-seven years to date.

~:~

The freshness of the thoughts of a
philosopher who lived a hundred
generations ago allow me to
almost believe in immortality.

~:~

The dimensions of a problem
change depending on the angle
from which it is viewed.

~:~

∾⦂∾

If you engage in magical
thinking and get results, you are
a true magician.

∾⦂∾

It isn't easy to accurately
describe anything without
comparing it to something else.

∾⦂∾

As a thinker I have no business,
profession or trade, but I do
have an occupation.

∾⦂∾

From Plato's Academy to the
Academy Awards — we still live in
darkness, watching the shadows cast
on the walls of the cave or the screen.

∾⦂∾

~:~

Anyone who has ever uttered
the phrase "you have my full
attention" is telling an untruth,
because there is no such thing.

~:~

No one thinks faster than a con
man, or slower than a philosopher.

~:~

I need to take time to think,
and that will take the remaining
days and years of my life.

~:~

I like to think that I'm writing for
readers as far in the future as the
first written words are behind me.

~:~

～:～

When we speak of being
philosophical about a misfortune, we
should mean that we have examined
its meaning, but more likely we just
mean that we are accepting our fate.

～:～

Wittgenstein missed the mark in saying that
language is the problem — the real problem
is that nobody is listening.

～:～

Nothing is really "thought
out," because all thought is
fragmentary and disjointed.

～:～

If I were the president of a university, the
first thing I would do is move the philosophy
department outdoors onto a porch.

～:～

∽:∼

One day an old philosopher woke up
saying, "I can't believe I've wasted my
entire life … thinking."

∽:∼

Philosophy should be a requirement
in all colleges, but it should be
strongly discouraged as a profession.

∽:∼

Distrust any philosophical notion that
cannot be stated in an aphorism.

∽:∼

Why am I so stupid even
though I'm a philosopher?

∽:∼

In the ancient world philosophers
were made to take poison —
now we kill them with tenure.

∽:∼

~:~

Any book of philosophy could
accurately be titled *Such Is Life*.

~:~

Philosophy is about the infinity of ways
to prove that we really know nothing,
although we have no alternative except to
act as if we do know something.

~:~

What have I learned that isn't
obviously the case?

~:~

⁓:⁓

Canada and Mexico wouldn't
mind sharing a common border.

⁓:⁓

The best way to keep your blood
pressure down is not to think about
the government very much.

⁓:⁓

Journalists have many ways of
reporting the news accurately
while slanting it.

⁓:⁓

❦

We Americans are always
talking about our freedoms, but
has there ever been a country
that has so many laws?

❦

The hard lessons of history
are easily forgotten.

❦

Having a dull ax to grind
will produce a few sparks
but very little light.

❦

A suicide bomber is a murderer
who simultaneously convicts
and executes himself.

❦

❦

I don't feel as bad about our
American democracy when I think
of the politicians who are in jail.

❦

The public always cheers the
beginning of a military solution.

❦

Four million people have died in the
war in the Congo, but a celebrity
displaying her panties getting out of
a limo is much bigger news.

❦

When you send your son to war
he becomes the property of the
nation — as in "our troops,"
"our veterans," "our wounded,"
and "our war dead."

❦

∽:∾

In the heart of an empire there
is little sense of the difference
between defense and conquest.

∽:∾

Democracies limp along because
the voters, though perpetually
disappointed, somehow manage
to remain hopeful.

∽:∾

As the election approaches our
mailboxes begin to fill with lies.

∽:∾

People who work for the government
tend to get defensive even when
you've said nothing against them.

∽:∾

~:~

How many people do you know who
can't discuss politics for two minutes
without beginning to rant?

~:~

You can't view politics
intelligently through the dirty
lens of an ideology.

~:~

If you don't believe that
millions are ready to die for
Islamism, think of the millions
who died for Fascism and for
Communism.

~:~

If their goal is to inconvenience us,
terrorists are winning the war.

~:~

~:~

If I had to do it all over again, I think
I would try to get rich before I tried
to overthrow the capitalist system,
rather than the other way around.

~:~

Is there a nation on earth in which
there is half as much passion about
politics as there is about sports?

~:~

Strange that the most patriotic people
hate and fear government the most.

~:~

Politicians are always looking
for the lowest common
denominator.

~:~

~:~

The problem for liberals is that
they give ground, but conservatives
seldom meet them halfway.

~:~

In times of national hysteria we
Americans clamber to give up our rights.

~:~

The volunteer army has taken
the wind out of the sails of the
anti-war movement.

~:~

Terrorists are to a state like the fleas
on a dog, they can make the dog
miserable, but they can't kill it.

~:~

❀

A mad ruler provokes an insane war
his country cannot win; a hundred
years later, historians offer theories
as to why the war was inevitable.

❀

In a place bustling with tourists from
many nations, it almost seems possible
that we could get along with each other.

❀

On the left you will find more
sympathy for criminals than you
will find in any prison.

❀

Obedience is not on any curriculum,
but it is taught everywhere.

❀

∽:∼

There are times when you
can learn more about what is
happening by reading history
than by reading the newspaper.

∽:∼

I am the American people, and I
don't need the liberal or conservative
media to tell me what my mood is.

∽:∼

We Americans do not like to let
our military get rusty.

∽:∼

American politics are a kind of
sexual tease — all promise and
no performance.

∽:∼

～:～

In America we select our candidates
through a process of destruction.

～:～

The average leftist would cringe
in a workingman's bar, where
flavorful speech is ornamented with
chauvinism, sexism, and bigotry.

～:～

It takes a lot of dying to maintain an
empire — and whether the benefits are
worth the cost depends on how close
you are to those doing the dying.

～:～

There is no point in criticizing
capitalism, because the alternatives
have turned out to be even worse.

～:～

⌒:∼

The less civilized people are the
more damage they can do with
their fists; and the more civilized
the more damage they can do
with their words.

⌒:∼

I don't see why people who
watch too many movies feel
superior to people who watch
too much television.

⌒:∼

Never use the slang of another
generation — you won't get it right.

⌒:∼

~:~

Chess, played seriously,
is a murderous game.

~:~

A lack of culture
shows through culture.

~:~

Cultural pride should be
confined to those characteristics
we would otherwise be proud of.

~:~

How is it that we're a nation of
immigrants who are so poor at
learning other languages?

~:~

It's easier to start a new clique
than to break into one.

~:~

～:～

One sign of progress is that
although travelers are still
cheated, they are rarely eaten.

～:～

Folklore isn't folklore
when it's your lore.

～:～

You can only believe in notions of
national character if you haven't
actually met many people from
the country in question.

～:～

Devotees of an esoteric interest often
have a low opinion of the devotees of
a slightly different esoteric interest.

～:～

~:~

We can easily dismiss an
ignorant bigot — but not so
easily an educated one.

~:~

As a Jew, permitted to eat
grasshoppers and forbidden to eat
shrimp, nothing other religions allow
or forbid seems odd to me.

~:~

Trying to view your own culture is
like trying to get a look at the pool in
which you are swimming.

~:~

The waltz was the dirty dancing
of the nineteenth century.

~:~

~:~

A culture of extreme individualism
and independence tends to
breed loneliness.

~:~

Scrabble players develop large
vocabularies, but not very useful ones.

~:~

In a high school, the cream of society
vanishes at the end of each school year.

~:~

I've never felt more useless as a
human being than as a tourist.

~:~

The troubles of the cities increase
because cities attract the troubled.

~:~

~:~

You may be a bourgeois,
but can you spell it?

~:~

The sad disappointment of
meeting bohemians is that most
of them are far less interesting
than they appear.

~:~

I'm at home in any home with walls
of books because I know that we'll
have things to talk about.

~:~

Tourists are a valuable resource, but
they must be carefully separated
from their money before being
shipped back to their country of
origin as finished goods.

~:~

༄༅

You needn't feel like a
prisoner of your ethnicity.

༄༅

Humans are logical creatures, but
not rational ones. This explains all
human relations and history.

༄༅

The locals are not going to tell
you the good fishing places.

༄༅

One has a sense of false security as
a tourist — as if no one would dare
harm you — and so tourists brag
about having walked confidently
around cities where it was just dumb
luck that they weren't mugged.

༄༅

∾∶∾

Cultural pride is good, but notions
of cultural superiority can
only cause harm.

∾∶∾

The problem isn't that we
Americans have so many guns;
the problem is our propensity to
shoot each other with them.

∾∶∾

Every culture has its cultural
excuses for bad behavior, and
they often come in handy.

∾∶∾

As tourists we spent far more than
we intended because the foreign
currencies were only play money.

∾∶∾

❦

Getting to know yourself is not
necessarily getting to like yourself.

❦

The only rule of the blame game
is to never accept it.

❦

In doling out forgiveness
based on remorse, one has
to take the remorse on faith.

❦

When you're trying to escape blame,
the simple truth suddenly becomes
very complicated.

❦

∾:∾

If you met yourself would you want
to be friends with this person?

∾:∾

The most entertaining version is
usually not the truest one.

∾:∾

It is easier to be brave when
cowardice is not an alternative.

∾:∾

The murder rate is nothing
compared to what it would be if
people could read minds.

∾:∾

Everyone has a story,
and also a back-story.

∾:∾

∼:∼

It is good for you to have a way
with words, but not good for
words to have a way with you.

∼:∼

Sarcasm lowers you,
but irony is elegant.

∼:∼

The fewer words you can say it
in, the better you have said it.

∼:∼

It's a lot easier to take credit
than to take responsibility.

∼:∼

Air quotes are a means of saying you
don't really mean what you are saying.

∼:∼

~:~

We enjoy the illusion that we're
dealing with something just because
it's been lingering on our to-do list.

~:~

My mind is held hostage
by my prejudices.

~:~

I have a talent for attempting
things that require more
talent than I have.

~:~

I often eat animals — oops —
I meant to say that I often eat meat.

~:~

I'd rather hear you say that I
have a juvenile sense of humor
than a geriatric one.

~:~

∾:∾

Ninety-eight percent of us have our true
character written on our foreheads — the
other two percent keep us on our guard.

∾:∾

You can't argue with nonsense
because talking sense to it just
elicits more nonsense.

∾:∾

Surprising how much we can tell from
other people's small eye movements.

∾:∾

If only we took as much care in
choosing our words as we do a shirt.

∾:∾

Living in a despotism people lose some
of their ability to discern what is true
because fear can shape even what we
allow ourselves to think.

∾:∾

~:~

You can hit the bull's-eye
with irony, but your sarcasm is
nothing more than a cheap shot.

~:~

You can fake many things, but not
eccentricity, because a true eccentric is
inexplicably, uniquely, insanely odd.

~:~

Excuses are leaky buckets that
by and large hold no water.

~:~

People justify the lives they have lived
in terms of things "they had to do,"
but in reality, there are very few things
in life that most people "had to do."

~:~

∽:∼

"It's complicated" may be true, but it is
neither an explanation nor an excuse.

∽:∼

It's best if the story you tell yourself
about your life has some relation to
the facts of the matter.

∽:∼

Insanity is believing anything you
can imagine; that is, insanity is a
triumph of imagination over reality.

∽:∼

You will always be just yourself,
which is disappointing — except
in your imagination, where the
possibilities are infinite.

∽:∼

~:~

An atheist imagines he will die
and that will be the end of him.
A believer imagines that he will die
and his immortal soul will live forever —
yet another proof that imagination
is a much finer thing than reality.

~:~

The illusion of having no illusions is
the greatest delusion of all.

~:~

Listen to the speaker with your
eyes as well as your ears, and
you will hear much more.

~:~

~:~

It's not often that a
novel novel appears.

~:~

Great sex, realistically depicted
in a film, would be totally boring
because it would seem so slow.

~:~

Lay words as a bricklayer lays
bricks, each where it should be.

~:~

I'm looking for poetry
that can change my life.

~:~

∾:∽

When I find exactly the right
word I feel like a miner who has
picked up a gold nugget.

∾:∽

This writer will desex his pronouns
when he desexes himself.

∾:∽

The thoughts and feelings of
the most ordinary people are
extraordinary when they are
conveyed by great writers.

∾:∽

Crime fiction is the easiest to
write because anything that can
be said about evil is plausible.

∾:∽

∾:∾

I just can't seem to find
time not to write.

∾:∾

You could learn everything you
need to know about human
nature the hard way — or
you could stay home and read
Shakespeare, Joyce, and Proust.

∾:∾

It is the frustrated actors
who never stop acting.

∾:∾

Proust was French and died
twenty years before I was born,
but I know him a lot better than
I know my neighbors.

∾:∾

~:~

There is something wonderful
about meeting people who
have read a book that you've
written — it's as if they have
traveled in your mind.

~:~

The less interesting a life you've
led, the harder you have to
work on your memoirs.

~:~

You couldn't tell the history of the
world in ten lines of prose, but you
could do it in ten lines of poetry.

~:~

It's not all that hard to write my
thousand words a day — as long as I
write my thousand words a day.

~:~

~:~

My ambition is modest —
to simply produce more culture
than I consume.

~:~

Creative hours need a lot of
empty space around them.

~:~

There is no way of teaching
originality, because it
has no method.

~:~

I write books — but I'm no
longer sure what books are.

~:~

In living the creative life, work is
always your best friend.

~:~

~:~

Give me life imitating art
anytime over art imitating life.

~:~

Being an artist is like lap
swimming — there are days
when you just don't feel like getting
in the water, but when you do
you're always glad you did.

~:~

Language is a tool, and like any tool,
it needs to be sharpened, calibrated,
lubricated, polished, and generally
kept in good order.

~:~

In the crossword puzzle universe,
Ned Rorem is a very great composer,
Mozart, insignificant.

~:~

⌒:∼

I sometimes feel as if I'm writing
myself into existence, the printed
words being mere documentation.

⌒:∼

The audience for poetry is about
equal to the number of living poets.

⌒:∼

Most fiction is as improbable
as science fiction.

⌒:∼

If you can't punctuate,
you can't think, in ink.

⌒:∼

Four hundred years and counting
and we're still waiting for that next
Shakespeare to come along.

⌒:∼

∽:∽

There is not much happiness in
literature because happiness has
very little narrative value.

∽:∽

I need poetry to keep me from
going completely sane.

∽:∽

We have words for every thing,
but not for every feeling.

∽:∽

The novel you can't put down is probably
a forgettable piece of skillfully written
trash wrapped around a clever plot.

∽:∽

"Museum-mind" is that reverential
state induced by art that has been
sanctified by museumification.

∽:∽

∼:∼

That most neglected, unappreciated
and seldom taught art —
the art of conversation.

∼:∼

A motionless heron stands
near the shore, waiting to spear
a passing fish, as I wait for a
thought, poised at my keyboard.

∼:∼

An artist gets a lot of mileage
out of a few words of praise.

∼:∼

Choosing poverty does not
simplify matters for the artist.

∼:∼

What the artist needs most is to become
afflicted with "enthousiasmos" —
inspired by a god.

∼:∼

❦

Great writing has you by the
throat in the first lines.

❦

We all go through life constantly
taking notes. Some write them
down. Those are called writers.

❦

The beauty of writing in a paper
notebook is that a notebook can't
go online and waste the time you
should have been working.

❦

Everybody imagines, but the artist
puts his imagination hard to work.

❦

We're all raised with a language, but
to become a serious artist you have
to invent your own language.

❦

~:~

Weirdness for its own sake is
never interesting, but interesting
things can be weird.

~:~

Can't imagine a better artist's
life than Emily Dickinson's —
she managed to just stay home
and do her creative work.

~:~

There's no such thing as writer's
block, because if you aren't
writing, you aren't a writer.

~:~

The rhythm of writing
is called punctuation —
language is the melody.

~:~

~:~

The nakedest truth is you,
naked, in front of your mirror.

~:~

There is a horror movie called,
My Face in the Washroom Mirror —
After Seven Hours on the Plane.

~:~

Our most comfortable clothes are
those that should be in the rag bin.

~:~

⌒:⌒

The single most valuable skill in
relationships and careers is the
ability to be gracefully
and ungrudgingly wrong.

⌒:⌒

On the Internet he was a
legend on his own page.

⌒:⌒

With the creation of the online
world, we have all become
stalkers, of ourselves.

⌒:⌒

The proudest ones are often the
most transparent failures.

⌒:⌒

∾:∾

A very fine ambition is to
simply be a nice person.

∾:∾

Is there a country in the world so poor
that it can't afford a presidential palace?

∾:∾

The curse of narcissism is that
everything reminds the narcissist of
something about himself — and so he
lacks the distance that makes it possible
to think clearly about anything.

∾:∾

There have been times in my life when I
should have judged myself harshly — but
there always seem to have been these
extenuating circumstances....

∾:∾

~:~

There are dance steps you can
do only in your dreams.

~:~

You will never see a photograph
of yourself that looks like the
self you imagine yourself to be.

~:~

A love for the sound of your
own voice — now there's a love
that never dies.

~:~

You can't persuade narcissists
that they are narcissistic because
they know that everything truly
is about them.

~:~

⌒:⌒

Sometimes my confidence is
shaken — other times beaten,
minced, chopped, whipped,
shredded, seared or macerated.

⌒:⌒

The shame has gone out of
shameless self-promotion.

⌒:⌒

In a hundred years I'll know
whether I became famous.

⌒:⌒

There are three kinds of
universes: my universe, your
universe, and the universe.

⌒:⌒

∼:∼

You don't need to put up a front if you
have a lot of money, or none at all.

∼:∼

God, sex, she, he, we, me, I —
why such tiny words for
such large matters?

∼:∼

The word "professor" makes me
think of something stuffed.

∼:∼

Men seldom have complicated
relationships with their faces.

∼:∼

∽:∼

Arriving late and making a
grand entrance gives one an
imaginary sense of importance.

∽:∼

The more highly educated you
are, the more likely you are to
suffer from delusions of being
highly intelligent.

∽:∼

Tell a narcissist about a famine
and he will tell you what he had
for breakfast.

∽:∼

Note to self: Self is not notable.

∽:∼

~:~

Your experiences are only interesting
if they are enhanced by
your sensibility.

~:~

An elegant suit makes a man
look pretty, but useless.

~:~

A pretty man and a handsome
woman make an attractive couple.

~:~

We meet ourselves, but not exactly
afresh, each morning in our mirrors.

~:~

~:~

Eventually, so many things that
seemed to matter so very much
turn out to hardly matter at all.

~:~

I still have the dream — the dream
that a day will come when once
again I shall fit into these pants.

~:~

Do you find the things you tell
people about yourself interesting
when other people tell you these
things about themselves?

~:~

⁓:⁓

It's the sure things that
turn out really badly.

⁓:⁓

Economists speak in numbers that
once were the province of astronomers.

⁓:⁓

A good restaurant meal for two
in your thirties is about equal to a
month of retirement in your seventies.

⁓:⁓

You are owned by your creditors.

⁓:⁓

~:~

Capitalism means freedom —
for those who have money.

~:~

Did you know that all of your debts
are assets — to your creditors?

~:~

If I became a billionaire the first
things I'd buy would be a giant
needle and a very small camel.

~:~

If you owe more than you have, even the
money in your wallet is borrowed.

~:~

⌒:∼

The makers of luxury goods feast on
the insecurities of the newly rich.

⌒:∼

Financial planning, for the
working majority, is about
finding ways to manage until the
next paycheck.

⌒:∼

Money is the lubricant of life,
and the more that is applied, the
smoother the ride.

⌒:∼

Imagine that you are rich —
then imagine that you aren't
any happier — that's life.

⌒:∼

≈∶≈

Money, which is actually a belief system,
was invented before capitalism and
it will outlast capitalism.

≈∶≈

Credit cards are the banker's
sweatshop — efficiently extracting
wealth from working people, and
with all the laws on their side.

≈∶≈

I watch all my investments, but I
have no idea what they are up to.

≈∶≈

Wherever easy money is promised,
there you will find the greatest
concentration of scoundrels.

≈∶≈

~:~

All financial advisers should be
required to provide their clients
with frequent statements of
their own personal finances.

~:~

You can ridicule the voodoo
economics of the Reagan era,
but studying the history of
economics, it seems as if it's all
voodoo economics.

~:~

Once you've decided to spend way
too much money on something, it's
not hard to spend even more on it.

~:~

∽:∼

The wishes of a major contributor
carry more weight than those of
many selfless volunteers.

∽:∼

There is a book that can
make many wonderful
things happen — it's called a
checkbook.

∽:∼

Being able to check one's
investments online at any hour
only adds to the anxiety level.

∽:∼

The dirty little secret of investing is that
the stock market is totally random.

∽:∼

∽:∼

Having money may not make
you happy, but it does alleviate
the anxiety of not having it.

∽:∼

With privilege, the list of what one
"can't bear" is likely to grow long —
but the poor can "bear" anything,
because they have no alternative.

∽:∼

The majority of careers fall into one
of two categories. The first is earning
money by providing a useful product or
service. The second is devising ways of
separating the first from their money.

∽:∼

New money ages rapidly, often becoming
old money in just one generation.

∽:∼

Business

_____

∾:∽

Lifetimes of hard work, loyalty
and dedication appear nowhere
on corporate balance sheets.

∾:∽

To learn the art of sales
from the masters, study the
televangelists who nightly sell
the promise of riches to those
who send them money.

∾:∽

If a Ponzi scheme were something
that occurred only in literature, it
would seem improbable.

∾:∽

⌒:∼

A landlord does not expect to be loved.

⌒:∼

Luck should be only the
minority partner in your life.

⌒:∼

Confidence is always
helpful — overconfidence isn't.

⌒:∼

More money is made from
brilliant imitation than from
brilliant innovation.

⌒:∼

Every vocation and hobby has its
parasites who infest every gathering
to shamelessly promote their
products and services.

⌒:∼

∼:∼

The profession of law attracts
some of the best and the worst
people in our society.

∼:∼

After my career in business I
wonder how many meetings, if
any, were necessary.

∼:∼

Success gurus offer little of value
in the real world, but what they are
actually selling is hope — and there
is always a seller's market for hope.

∼:∼

A very successful business career
can turn on just one great
idea, decision or deal.

∼:∼

∾⁝∾

A real estate bubble, or any other
bubble, goes along pretty well until
all the suckers are fully invested.

∾⁝∾

There are shameless self-promoters
who make their livings promoting
shameless self-promotion —
where will it all end?

∾⁝∾

Doctors have patients, lawyers
clients, priests parishioners, rabbis
congregants, mayors citizens —
but these are all just names
for customers.

∾⁝∾

When someone offers me business
advice I'm always curious to know
how much business they are doing.

∾⁝∾

The art of managing people is largely
the art of managing expectations.

~:~

The landlord has a lot more to
worry about than the tenant,
but few would rather be the
tenant than the landlord.

~:~

The executive must have an ability to
survive and even appear comfortable
in a business suit under conditions of
high heat and humidity.

~:~

The reason for most business training is
that employees are too lazy to read.

~:~

∽:∽

A downward career generates
its own momentum.

∽:∽

A mechanic has
intelligent hands.

∽:∽

America is a country with a good-
sized middle class, and a much larger
working class who have been led to
believe that they belong to it.

∽:∽

∾:∾

Your list of things that are
worth having to work hard for
should be very short.

∾:∾

Working with adults, you can tell
who was the schoolyard bully.

∾:∾

Part of the unemployment rate is a
certain constant, which we could call
the unemployable rate.

∾:∾

There are times when the average
house cleaner has more job security
than the average senior manager.

∾:∾

∾:∾

A newly promoted boss suffers
from an illusion of control.

∾:∾

Everyone needs two in-boxes:
Consequences and
No Consequences.

∾:∾

The cocktail hour makes for
a pleasant transition from the
day's work to the evening's work.

∾:∾

Contrary to conservative
propaganda, the vast majority
of Americans are, and always
will be, working class.

∾:∾

~:~

The first rule of troubleshooting
is to make no assumptions.

~:~

We are almost pathetically
grateful for competence when
we encounter it.

~:~

Saving the unpleasant task for last
just adds dread to the rest of the day.

~:~

I'm looking for some evidence
that there is a correlation between
being good at job interviews
and being good at jobs.

~:~

～:～

When it comes to fixing things, my
hands are smarter than my brain.

～:～

Have you noticed that the less
you have on your calendar,
the more you get done?

～:～

A deadline creates energy that did
not exist in the universe before.

～:～

Salaried employees feel superior to
hourly workers, even when doing less
skilled work, and for less money.

～:～

❦

The controlling personality finds
it hard to believe that other people
know how to do their work.

❦

Someone described himself to me
as "Retired from never having had
a career." I wondered what's the
retirement age for that?

❦

Losing your job at thirty is an
inconvenience, at forty a setback,
after fifty an absolute disaster.

❦

Some of us change careers until
we discover our true vocations —
and some until we're too old to work.

❦

⌒:∼

Flurries of calls and emails create the
illusion that things are happening.

⌒:∼

You can lose years of credit for doing
good work by trying to shift blame
for the one occasion when you didn't.

⌒:∼

If we paid teachers like lawyers, and
lawyers like teachers, we would have
a more decent society.

⌒:∼

There are overconfident, smart
people who never make a career
breakthrough because they
won't seek advice or mentoring.

⌒:∼

~:~

Never let a job become your identity.

~:~

Pretending to have a career
has dignity, but you can hardly
make a living from it.

~:~

If you grew up knowing what you wanted
to do with your life, there's a good
probability you will achieve that career.

~:~

Hard work is honorable, but hard
thinking will take you a lot farther in life.

~:~

~:~

Foremost amongst the ranks of
the incompetent are those who are
always saying, "I know, I know."

~:~

The A+ student is probably not
going to invent the thing that
will change the world — but he
will make an excellent employee.

~:~

In school, and later in our careers,
we generally find that authority
favors obedience over originality.

~:~

Truth filters are implanted
in the ears of law students.

~:~

Suggested Reading

The page of my website (ithoughtso.net) titled "I Sit at the Feet of the Masters" (http://ithoughtso.net/id11.html) is a large collection of my favorite quotations, and a good place to encounter the names of great aphorists. Previously, I've offered a short list of books, but there are now so many quotation websites that the best way to gain a quick familiarity with the greatest aphorists is to search by name, so I will merely offer a short list of those I have found most useful or entertaining.

La Rochefoucauld, Schopenhauer, Epictetus, Oscar Wilde, Mark Twain, Samuel Johnson, Cicero, Bertrand Russell, Zeno of Citium, William Blake, Wittgenstein, Diogenes, Heraclitus, Marcus Aurelius, Seneca, Rousseau, Montaigne, Nietzsche, Warhol, John Cage, Lichtenberg, Thoreau, William Burroughs, Bukowski, Dorothy Parker, Dr. Seuss, Philip Larkin, Orwell, Jesus, Confucius, Einstein, Franklin, Will Rogers, Mae West, Goethe, Pascal, Mencken, Swift, Shaw, Voltaire, McLuhan, Picasso, Cocteau, Van Gogh, Flaubert, Rumi, Bob Dylan, Banksy, Groucho Marx, Socrates, Lewis Carroll, Gertrude Stein, Calvin Trillin, Artaud, Malraux, Hegel, Zizek, Kafka, John Waters, Frank Zappa, Plato, Maurice Sendak, and James Joyce.

There is an excellent bibliography in *The World in a Phrase* by James Geary (Bloomsbury, 2005).

About the Author

Michael Lipsey lives in San Rafael, California, and is always happy to hear from readers. *The Quotable Stoic* is his third collection of original aphorisms.

Contact: mike@ithoughtso.net

Web: ithoughtso.net

Index